TRAINS

Jean Coppendale

School Specialty
Publishing

Columbus, Ohio

This edition published in the United States in 2009 by Brighter Child, an imprint of School Specialty Publishing, a member of the School Specialty Family.

Send inquiries to:
School Specialty Publishing
8720 Orion Place
Columbus, Ohio 43240

www.SchoolSpecialtyPublishing.com

ISBN 0-7696-5793-1
ISBN 13: 978-0-7696-5793-6
Part Number: M00000997

Copyright © QEB Publishing, Inc. 2007

First published in the United States by
QEB Publishing, Inc.
23062 La Cadena Drive
Laguna Hills, CA 92653

www.qeb-publishing.com

Written by Jean Coppendale
Designed by Chhaya Sajwan (Q2A Media)
Editor Katie Bainbridge
Picture Researcher Lalit Dalal (Q2A Media)

Publisher Steve Evans
Creative Director Zeta Davies
Senior Editor Hannah Ray

Printed and bound in China.

Picture credits
Key: t = top, b = bottom, c = center,
l = left, r = right, FC = front cover, BC = back cover
Joe Osciak: with thanks for image on page 4–5
SBB AG, Bern - Fotodienst/Alain D. Boillat: 5
Jtb Photo Communications Inc/Photolibrary: 6–7, 19
The Glacier Express: 7 t: Louie Schoeman: 8–9
CORBIS: Paul A. Souders 9 t
Dave Toussaint Photography: 10–11, 20–21
Paul Lantz: 11 b: ALSTOM Transport: 12–13
Denis Baldwin: 14–15
Alamy: Gunter Marx 16–17, Peter Titmuss 17 t
Photo by Fred Guenther: 18–19
Getty: Bruce Hands FC, Lloyd Park BC

Table of Contents

Words in **bold** can be found in the glossary.

What Is a Train?

Trains are used to carry people from one place to another. They also carry **goods**, such as cars and coal. A train has special wheels that allow it to move along tracks.

Some trains carry **passengers** from one city to another.

There is a **cab** at the front of a train. This is where the driver sits and makes the train start and stop.

Train Travel

Trains can travel anywhere there are tracks. They can climb mountains and speed across large areas of land. Trains travel over water on bridges and under water through **tunnels**.

Sometimes, trains travel through beautiful countrysides.

In Switzerland, trains travel through mountains covered with snow.

In some places, trains travel through tunnels that are cut into the mountains. Tunnels are made if the mountains are too high or too steep for trains to climb.

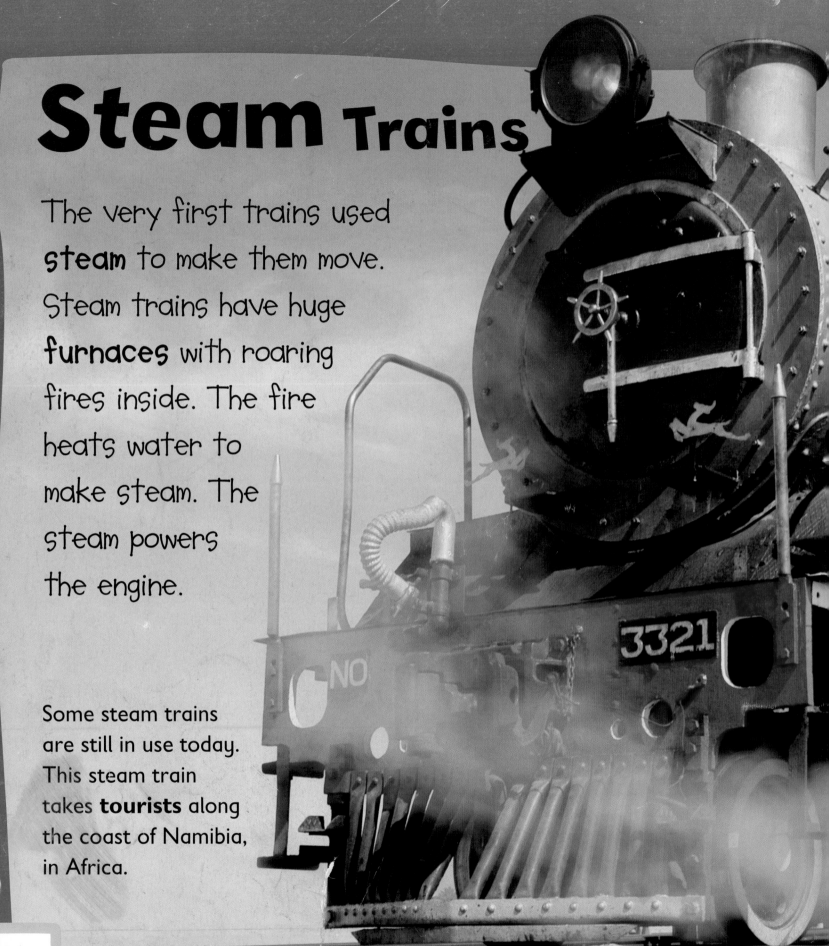

Steam Trains

The very first trains used **steam** to make them move. Steam trains have huge **furnaces** with roaring fires inside. The fire heats water to make steam. The steam powers the engine.

Some steam trains are still in use today. This steam train takes **tourists** along the coast of Namibia, in Africa.

The furnace is at the front of the train. Workers shovel coal into the furnace throughout the journey to keep the train moving.

Keeping the fires burning is a dirty job. It's also a very hot job!

Freight Trains

Freight, or **cargo**, trains are used to carry different **loads** from one place to another. It is cheaper and faster to transport big, heavy loads by train than by other vehicles.

A train with lots of freight cars can carry huge loads across the country. These cars can also make the train very long!

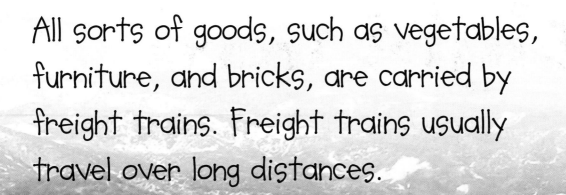

All sorts of goods, such as vegetables, furniture, and bricks, are carried by freight trains. Freight trains usually travel over long distances.

This freight train is carrying new cars to a car dealer.

Everyday Trains

Some trains take people to work in the morning and bring them home again in the evening. They are called **commuter trains**. Commuter trains can get crowded during **rush hour**. Sometimes there are not enough seats for everyone. Some people have to stand in the aisle and hold onto poles.

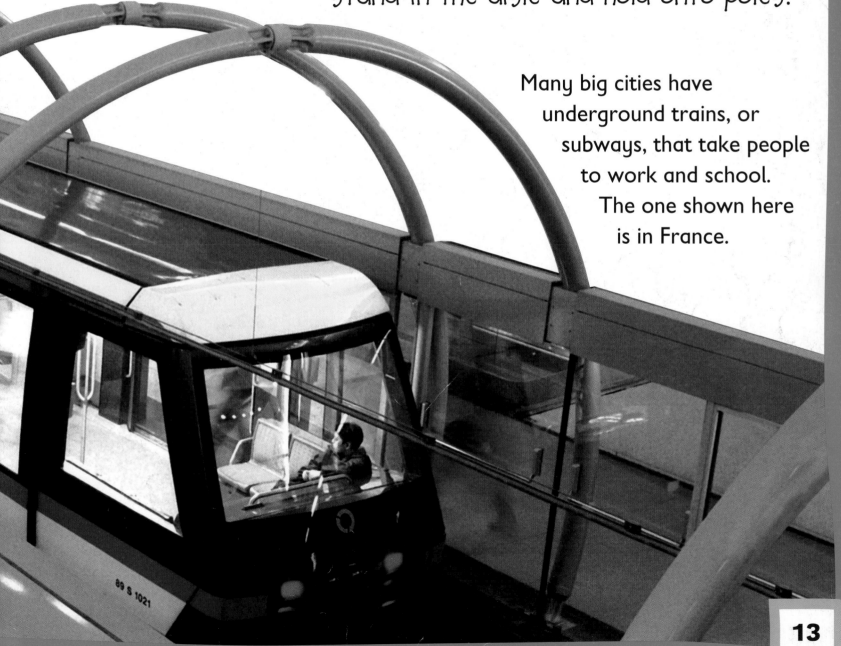

Many big cities have underground trains, or subways, that take people to work and school. The one shown here is in France.

89 S 1021

Monorails and Skytrains

Some trains travel high above the ground. They are called monorails and skytrains. They move people short distances very quickly. Monorails move on one track. Skytrains move on two tracks. They are useful in busy places where there are a lot of people. Many airports and **amusement parks** have them.

This skytrain is in Detroit, Michigan. It does not have a driver because it is controlled by a computer.

This is a Maglev monorail. It does not have wheels. Instead, it moves using magnets.

Water—No Problem!

Trains are heavy, so a bridge carrying a train has to be very strong.

Big bridges are built over lakes and rivers so trains can travel across water. Some bridges have both a road and train tracks. Cars and trains can cross these bridges at the same time.

Some trains travel under the water. They go through special tunnels.

The Channel Tunnel in Europe is one of the longest undersea tunnels in the world. It has shuttles that take people and vehicles back and forth between England and France.

Express Trains

Some trains quickly carry passengers long distances. These are called express trains. They stop at only a few stations and travel very fast.

This tilting train travels very fast.

Some express trains can **tilt** slightly when they go around **curves** on the track. This is so they do not have to slow down.

Some trains have huge windows and a glass roof. Passengers can enjoy the view as they travel!

Sleeper Cars

Some passenger trains have to travel long distances through the night. These trains have special **cars** called sleeper cars. In sleeper cars, passengers stay in a room called a **cabin** where they can sleep and even take showers!

These kinds of trains also have a restaurant on board where people can eat.

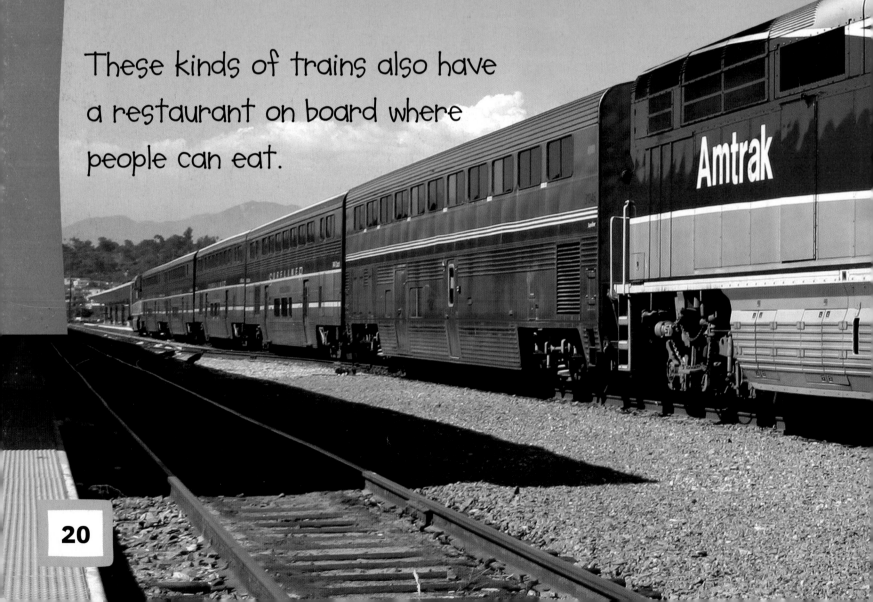

Some train trips last for days so it is important that passengers have a comfortable bed to sleep on while traveling.

Activities

- Make a train book. Collect pictures of trains from magazines. Write the names and descriptions of each train. Make a log of when and where you see each train.

- Look at the train below. What kind of train do you think it is?

- Make up a story about a train. What kind of train is it? Where is it going? What is it carrying? What happens during the trip?

- Have you ever been on a train? Where were you going? Who were you with? Draw a picture of yourself riding in a train.

- Look at the three pictures below. Which one shows train tracks?

  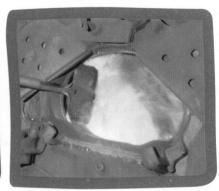

Glossary

amusement parks
Parks with rides, games, and food.

cab
The place where a driver sits.

cabin
A room in a sleeper car where passengers stay.

cargo
Items carried from one place to another. Also called freight.

cars
The parts of a train where passengers sit.

commuter trains
Trains that take people to and from their place of work.

curves
Lines that bend.

freight
Items carried from one place to another. Also called cargo.

furnaces
The places where fires burn to make steam for the train's engine.

goods
Things that are bought and sold.

loads
A large amount of something that is carried from one place to another.

passengers
People who pay to travel.

rush hour
The time of the day when large numbers of people travel to and from work.

steam
The foggy-looking puffs made when water is boiled.

tilt
When something leans to one side.

tourists
People who travel for pleasure.

tunnels
Underground passageways.

Index